Seahorses

Leo Statts

abdopublishing.com

Published by Abdo Zoom™, PO Box 398166, Minneapolis, Minnesota 55439. Copyright © 2017 by Abdo Consulting Group, Inc. International copyrights reserved in all countries. No part of this book may be reproduced in any form without written permission from the publisher. Abdo Zoom™ is a trademark and logo of Abdo Consulting Group, Inc.

Printed in the United States of America, North Mankato, Minnesota
092016
012017

THIS BOOK CONTAINS
RECYCLED MATERIALS

Cover Photo: Vladimir Wrangel/Shutterstock Images
Interior Photos: iStockphoto, 1, 4, 5, 8, 10–11, 12, 13, 19; Adam Lazar/iStockphoto, 7; Shutterstock Images, 9, 16; Red Line Editorial, 11, 20 (left), 20 (right), 21 (left), 21 (right); Laura Dinraths/Shutterstock Images, 15; Rich Carey/Shutterstock Images, 17; Elena Frolova/Shutterstock Images, 18–19

Editor: Brienna Rossiter
Series Designer: Madeline Berger
Art Direction: Dorothy Toth

Publisher's Cataloging-in-Publication Data
Names: Statts, Leo, author.
Title: Seahorses / by Leo Statts.
Description: Minneapolis, MN : Abdo Zoom, 2017. | Series: Ocean animals |
     Includes bibliographical references and index.
Identifiers: LCCN 2016948674 | ISBN 9781680799149 (lib. bdg.) |
     ISBN 9781624025006 (ebook) | ISBN 9781624025563 (Read-to-me ebook)
Subjects: LCSH: Seahorses--Juvenile literature.
Classification: DDC 597/.6798--dc23
LC record available at http://lccn.loc.gov/2016948674

Table of Contents

Seahorses

Seahorses are fish. There are more than 30 types of seahorses. They come in many sizes.

They use their tails
to hold on to plants.

Body

A **fin** on a seahorse's back helps it swim. A seahorse has two other small fins. One fin is on each side of its head.

These fins
help it steer.

Seahorses can change colors.

This helps them blend in with their environments.

Habitat

Seahorses live in warm oceans. You can find them in **shallow** water.

Seahorses are not very good swimmers.

They often travel by holding on to pieces of floating seaweed.

Food

Seahorses eat **plankton**.
A seahorse does not have teeth.
It does not have a stomach.
It needs to eat very often.

Its long **snout** sucks in food.

Life Cycle

Seahorses lay eggs.
Male seahorses have a pouch.

They carry
eggs inside
the pouch.
No other
male animals
do this.

17

Seahorses are on their own
after they are born.

They live for one to five years.

Smallest Length

A Satomi's pygmy seahorse is shorter than a penny.

0.5 in   0.75 in

Largest Length

A big-bellied seahorse is longer than a basketball.

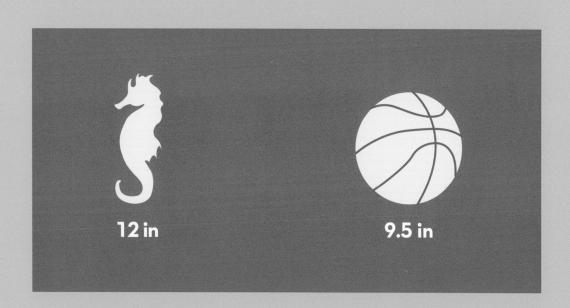

12 in   9.5 in

Glossary

environment - everything that surrounds and affects a living thing.

fin - a body part of a water animal that is shaped like a blade or fan.

plankton - very small animals that drift through the ocean.

pouch - a fold of skin.

shallow - not deep.

snout - a part of the face that sticks out. It has the nose and mouth.

Booklinks

For more information
on **seahorses**, please visit
booklinks.abdopublishing.com

Z m In on Animals!

Learn even more with the Abdo Zoom
Animals database. Check out
abdozoom.com for more information.

Index